# The Misadventures of David

## C is for Chicken Poop

ISBN: 978-81-19228-72-0

First Edition: 2023
Rs. 200/-

Cyberwit.net
HIG 45 Kaushambi Kunj, Kalindipuram
Allahabad - 211011 (U.P.) India
http://www.cyberwit.net
Tel: +(91) 9415091004
E-mail: info@cyberwit.net



Printed at VCORRE PRESS.

*Dedicated to my dad. For some unknown reason you have decided to use my writing skills for therapy for your crazy childhood antics and memories.*

# The Misadventures of David: C is for Chicken Poop

Written by

Loni Hoots

Illustrated by

Melissa Rohr

For some, car rides are not that exciting. Nothing happens, and once they reach the destination, everything usually goes to plan...but not for our young protagonist, David. Today, he is being put into a car with his dad, and grandpa, with their destination to visit his grandma's grave in another state.

While it is a somber moment for the trio as they are preparing to remember the great life of their loved one, they will soon find out that this trip is anything but somber.

It's early morning, yet, it is already getting hot, and no one is comfortable in the car. David's dad and grandpa have already begun to bicker, but in a loving manner about the stops along the way; the most important stop, where to get lunch later that day.

Several hours have passed, and David is sitting in the back seat trying to make the ride enjoyable, while his dad and grandpa make sense of the directions on the map. It's the early 80s so everything is completely different; no technology telling you when to turn, just you and a paper map that you have to keep out of the glove box in case the driver misses the exit. Certainly a time that many will remember, while others will never know the stress of.

“I’m getting hungry,” Grandpa announces.

David and his dad agree with this sentiment,
making it obvious that is now lunch time,
and their stomachs are grumbling from having
very little food since the beginning of the trip.

“Let’s get burgers,” David’s dad says.

“No, I want chicken.”

While they continue to argue over what to get,
David can’t get a word in, making him an audience
to the performance up in the front seats of the car.
Chicken or burgers, David didn’t care, this was a
treat for him while they were on this trip, which was
more than ten hours long.

After several minutes of bickering, Grandpa and David's dad settle on getting some chicken, but not *any* chicken, the holy grail of fast-food chicken, KFC. As soon as he is able, David's dad spots the chicken restaurant and pulls into the parking lot where they decide on getting a large bucket that they will eat out of during the rest of the trip. All three do not realize how badly this will end. A hot day and greasy fried food should never go hand in hand, and our little protagonist David will learn this and remember it for the rest of his life.

Being as small as he is, David sits in the back seat with the bucket of chicken beside him, giving his dad and grandpa pieces when they ask for them. At the same time, he helps himself to as much as he is able to stand. This will be his undoing.
Just a few more hours and they will reach their destination, but David might not make it till then, because the chicken he just ate had a strange reaction to his body, making him poop his pants.

His dad and grandpa haven't noticed what has happened, nor can they smell what has just occurred in the back seat, but they certainly will know by tomorrow morning.

It has now been several hours, and the three travelers have made it to their destination for the night. They are able to get inside the house and sleep on beds before seeing Grandma's gravestone the next day; but David is having a slight problem, and doesn't want anyone to know, because he's embarrassed and doesn't want to get into trouble.

“Head upstairs,” his great aunt says.
“That’s where you and your dad will sleep tonight.
Grandpa will sleep in the bedroom over here.”

David's dad settles into bed, telling him to hurry up so they are able to get some sleep because they have to get up early in the morning once again. But David can't hurry up, because something has gone terribly wrong in the bathroom.

Not only has he pooped his pants because of the greasy chicken he ate earlier, but he has clogged the toilet and it won't flush!

"Come on, flush!" he whispers to himself as he keeps trying to flush the toilet.

"David, time for bed." His dad says, trying to get his attention.

"Coming." David says after a few minutes, giving up on flushing the toilet.

Panicking, David tries to think quickly. He turns out the bathroom light and listens to his dad telling him to climb over him to get to the other side. Doing what he is told, David finds himself being settled into bed where he is able to fall asleep within a few minutes, even if he is still wearing his dirty pants.

Morning time is here, the sun is now peeking through the window, and David is being awakened by the sound of someone retching. It's his dad. His dad has found poop all over himself, and the toilet. It seems that David hasn't gotten rid of all of it, and instead it made its way onto his dad.

Within a matter of minutes, David is taken out of the bed and being searched. There was poop glued to his butt cheeks, making his pants stick to him. More retching sounds come from his dad, but then he is told to get downstairs because they would soon be leaving.

"Will I get to take a shower?" David wondered.

Nope, he wouldn't, because they hadn't had any extra clothing and were on a tight schedule.

The three of them got to see grandma's grave and got to send her loving thoughts to the heavens, hoping she receives them; even if one of them was squirming in his pants because he still had some poop residue left in them!

The car ride back home was a long one, indeed, and David is eager to get in the shower again, and into clean clothes; most importantly, hoping that he never sees the ones he was in ever again!

## About the Author

**Loni Hoots** is the author of twelve books including the children's book series, *The Little Bird Series*, which follows a young red bird named Little Bird along with all of his friends. As of 2022, she has had six poetry collections published through Middle Island Press, along with two novellas: *If You're Gonna Be There* and *Petals and Nails*, both receiving positive reviews. Since Spring 2022, she has been published through Cyberwit.net.

Her debut novel, *Secrets of Edenfield*, was re-released as a second edition for Kindle in Autumn 2022, and in paperback and hardback in Winter 2023.

## About the Illustrator

**Melissa** has a BFA in illustration through Columbia College Chicago (IL). She enjoys creating cute sea critter and animal illustrations in watercolor, pen, and colored pencil. Past illustrated book releases include *Little Bird, Little Bird* by Loni Hoots, *The Sleep Catcher* by Za Goodbrake, *Duskie the Owl* by Matthew Gindling, and a line of coloring books. Melissa is currently located in Fort Myers, Florida where she attends local art markets and enjoys freelance illustration projects. When Melissa is not making artwork, she enjoys practicing yoga, attending concerts, and exploring the beaches and trails of Southwest Florida.

www.ingramcontent.com/pod-product-compliance
Lightning Source LLC
Chambersburg PA
CBHW061316170726
48282CB00020B/117
* 9 7 8 8 1 1 9 2 2 8 7 2 0 *